Foxworthy's Pie Cookbook

A Little Slice of Heaven

Table of Contents

APPLE PIE

Ingredients for Pie:
1 brown paper bag
1 deep dish unbaked pie shell
5 grannie smith apples
1 cup sugar
1/8 teaspoon salt
1 tablespoon cinnamon
5 tablespoons all purpose flour
3 tablespoons water

Ingredients for Top Crust:
1 cup sugar
1 cup all purpose flour
2 sticks butter

Directions for Pie:
  Preheat the oven to 425 degrees. Peel and decore all apples; cut into slices.Place sliced apples into pie shell.Sprinkle sugar, salt, cinnamon, flour and water on apples.

Directions for Crust:
  In a small mixing bowl, combine sugar, flour and butter and mix with your hands.Sprinkle the crust mixture on top of the entire pie. Place pie in brown paper bag and staple shut.Bake for 1 hour.

Note: Double the top crust ingredients if needed for more crust.

BLACKBERRY PIE

Ingredients:
2 pie crusts
1/2 cup heavy cream
6 cups blackberries
1 cup sugar
1 ½ tablespoons clearjel
1/8 teaspoon salt

Directions:
   Preheat oven to 400 degrees. Place one pie crust in pie plate and form bottom crust and brush with heavy cream. Place blackberries into pie shell.Sprinkle sugar, clear jel, and salt on blackberries.Place the other pie crust on top, seal to the other crust and brush with heavy cream. Cut three slits in the middle of pie crust. Bake for 40 minutes.

Note:
Raspberries can be substituted for the blackberries.
Clear jel substitutions:1 ½ tablespoons clear jel = 1 tablespoon cornstarch

COCONUT CREAM PIE

Ingredients:
1 regular pie crust
2 packages coconut cream Jello pudding
2 packages dream whip
½ bag (14oz) coconut (toasted)
1 cup cold milk
1 teaspoon vanilla

Directions:
  Bake pie crust in oven at 350 degrees for 10 minutes and cool completely. Place coconut on a baking sheet and toast until lightly brown.Make pudding according to Jello package.Add half of the toasted coconut to pudding mixture.Put mixture into pie crust.

  To make whipped topping, combine 2 packages of dream whip, milk and vanilla in a medium mixing bowl.Beat for 4 to 5 minutes until topping has thickened and formed peaks.Place whipped topping on top of the pudding mixture.Garnish with other half of the coconut.Chill in the refrigerator for at least 1 hour.

NUTTY BUDDY PIES

Ingredients:
1 (8oz) package cream cheese, softened
1 cup milk
2 cups confectioner's sugar
2/3 cup crunchy peanut butter
2 cups frozen whipped topping, thawed
3 (9 inch) prepared Graham cracker crusts
¾ cups chocolate syrup
1 cup chopped salted peanuts

Directions:
In a large bowl, beat the cream cheese and milk until blended.Mix in the sugar and peanut butter until smooth.Fold in the whipped topping.Spoon mixture into all three Graham cracker crusts. (You can substitute chocolate cookie crusts for a different flavor)Drizzle each pie with chocolate syrup and sprinkle peanuts on top. Cover and freeze for at least three hours.Remove from the freezer 15minutes before serving.

CHOCOLATE CHESS PIE

Ingredients:
 1 stick butter
3 tablespoons cocoa
1 cup sugar
2 eggs, beaten
1 teaspoon vanilla
1 unbaked pie crust

Directions:
  Preheat oven to 350 degrees.In a medium pot, melt butter and add cocoa, mix well.Stir in sugar, eggs and vanilla.Pour into the pie crust and bake for 30 to 35 minutes.

GERMAN CHOCOLATE PIE

Ingredients:
2 unbaked pie shells
1 ½ cup sugar
1 ½ tablespoons flour
½ cup butter
pinch of salt
1 ½ tablespoons cocoa
3 eggs
1 cup evaporated milk
1 teaspoon vanilla extract
½ cup chopped pecans
1 cup coconut

Directions:
Preheat oven to 350 degrees.In a large mixing bowl, mix together sugar, flour, butter, salt, cocoa, eggs, evaporated milk and vanilla.Add in the pecans and coconut and mix well.Pour mixture into the pie shells and bake for 45 minutes.

TRANSPARENT PIE

Ingredients:
1 pie unbaked pie shell
4 eggs
2 cups sugar
1 stick butter, melted
4 tablespoons Karo (white) syrup
2 tablespoons vanilla
½ teaspoon salt
1 teaspoon apple cider vinegar

Directions:
Preheat oven to 375 degrees.In a small bowl, whisk eggs and set aside.In a medium pot over medium heat, melt butter and sugar together until smooth. Add in Karo syrup, vanilla, salt and vinegar. Add in eggs and stir constantly until mixed. (Don't let eggs scramble) Pour mixture into unbaked pie shell.Cook for 30 to 35 minutes until golden brown.Let pie cool before serving.

DERBY PIE

Directions:
¼ cup butter
1 cup sugar
3 eggs, beaten
¾ cup corn syrup
¼ teaspoon salt
1 teaspoon vanilla
½ cup semi-sweet chocolate
½ cup walnuts
2 tablespoons bourbon (optional)
1 unbaked pie shell

Directions:
 Preheat oven to 375 degrees. In a medium mixing bowl, cream butter and sugar together.Add in eggs and mix together.Then add the corn syrup, salt, vanilla, chocolate, walnuts and bourbon and mix well.Pour into the pie shell and bake for 45 minutes.

PECAN PIE

Ingredients:
1/3 cup butter, melted
1 cup sugar
1 cup light corn syrup
½ teaspoon salt
2 teaspoons vanilla
4 eggs
1 cup chopped pecans
1 unbaked pie shell

Directions:
Preheat oven to 375 degrees. In a medium mixing bowl, combine butter, sugar, corn syrup, salt and vanilla, beat well. Add in eggs one at a time and beat well, then add in pecans. Pour into the pie shell and bake for 40 to 45 minutes.

PUMPKIN PIE

Ingredients:
2 eggs
2 cups pumpkin (16oz can)
¾ cup granulated sugar
½ cup brown sugar
½ teaspoon salt
2 teaspoons cinnamon
½ teaspoon ginger
½ teaspoon nutmeg
¼ teaspoon cloves
1 can evaporated milk
1 unbaked pie shell

Directions:
Preheat oven to 425 degrees.In a large mixing bowl, beat eggs lightly.Stir in pumpkin, granulated sugar, brown sugar, salt, cinnamon, ginger, nutmeg, cloves and milk.Pour mixture into pie shell and bake for 15 minutes.Then, reduce temperature to 350 degrees and bake for 25 to 30 minutes.

PEANUT BUTTER PIE

Ingredients:
1 (8oz) package cream cheese, softened
2 cups powdered sugar
1 (16oz) container frozen whipped topping, thawed
12 oz creamy peanut butter
1 deep dish graham cracker crust
10 to 15 mini peanut butter cups, chopped

Directions:
In a large mixing bowl, beat cream cheese and sugar together.Add in the peanut butter and mix until smooth.Fold in half of the whipped topping.Place mixture into graham cracker crust.Top the pie with remaining whipped topping and sprinkle with peanut butter cups.Chill for 3 to 4 hours before serving.

SOUR CREAM LEMON PIE

Directions:
1 cup sugar
3 ½ tablespoons cornstarch
1 tablespoon lemon grind, grated
½ cup fresh lemon juice
3 egg yolks, lightly beaten
1 cup milk
¼ cup butter
1 cup sour cream
1 baked pie shell
1 cup heavy whipping cream, whipped
Lemon twists for garnishing

Ingredients:
Preheat oven to 350 degrees and bake pie shell for 10 minutes.In a medium saucepan over medium heat combine sugar, cornstarch, lemon grind, lemon juice, egg yolks and milk and stir until thick.Stir in butter and cool mixture to room temperature.Stir in sour cream then pour into pie shell.Cover pie with whipped cream and garnish with lemon twists.

SWEET POTATO PIE

Ingredients:
1 large sweet potato (about 1 lb)
½ cup butter softened
1 cup white sugar
2 eggs
½ cup milk
½ teaspoon nutmeg
½ teaspoon cinnamon
1 teaspoon vanilla
¼ teaspoon salt
1 unbaked pie crust

Directions:
Preheat oven to 350 degrees.In small saucepan, pour water to cover the potato and bring to a boil.Reduce heat and cook until tender.Drain water and place potato on a plate and mash.Let cool to room temperature.

In a medium bowl, cream butter and sugar together.Add eggs and mix well.Next, add milk, sweet potato,nutmeg, cinnamon, vanilla and salt and beat until smooth.Pour mixture into pie shell and bake for 35 to 40 minutes.Cool completely before serving.

ICE BOX PIE

Ingredients:
1 (12oz) container cool whip
1 can crushed pineapple (drained)
1 can condensed milk
1/3 cup lemon juice
1 cup chopped pecans
2 Graham cracker pie crusts

Directions:
In a medium bowl, blend cool whip, pineapple and milk together.Add lemon juice and pecans.Pour mixture into pie shells and refrigerate for 6 hours or overnight.

BANANA CREAM PIE

Ingredients:
1 (9inch) pie crust
¾ cup white sugar
1/3 cup all purpose flour
¼ teaspoon salt
2 ½ cups milk
3 egg yolks, beaten
2 tablespoons butter
1 ¾teaspoon vanilla extract
1 package dream whip
3 to 4 bananas
chocolate curls or shavings (optional)

Directions:
   Preheat oven to 350 degrees.Bake pie shell for 10 to 12 minutes.Cool completely.

Pudding Mixture:
   In a medium saucepan, over medium heat, combine the sugar, flour, and salt and mix well. Slowly add in the 2 cups of milk and stir constantly for 4 minutes until mixture is bubbly.Add in the egg yolks and stir for 2 to 3 minutes until mixture thickens.Remove from the saucepan from the stove and add in butter and 1 ¼ teaspoon vanilla.Stir until mixture has a smooth consistency.Let mixture cool for 15 minutes.

Whipped Topping:

In a mixing bowl, combine dream whip, ½ cup milk and ½ teaspoon vanilla extract.Beat on high for 4 to 5 minutes until topping thickens and form peaks.

Slice two bananas into small pieces and place in the bottom of the pie shell.Pour pudding mixture on top of bananas.Place whipped topping on top of the pudding mixture.Chill in the refrigerator for at least 2 hours.Before serving add one sliced banana and chocolate curls for garnishing.

Note: You may add a sliced banana into the pudding mixture for a more banana flavor.

PEACHES & CREAM PIE

Ingredients for Crust:
¾ cup flour
1 teaspoon baking powder
1 large package dry vanilla instant pudding (3.4 oz)
3 tablespoons butter
1 egg
½ cup milk
2 cups of fresh peaches (peeled and sliced)
1 pie crust

Directions for Crust:
 Preheat oven to 350 degrees.In a medium mixing bowl, combine flour, baking powder, vanilla pudding, butter, egg and milk together; mix well.Pour mixture into a 9" greased pie plate.Spread mixture on bottom and up all sides of the pan.Arrange peaches in pie crust neatly.

Ingredients for Topping:
3 oz cream cheese
¼ cup sugar
1 ½ tablespoon squeezed peach juice (squeeze juice from peelings)
1 tablespoon sugar
½ teaspoon cinnamon

Directions for Topping

In a medium mixing bowl, combine cream cheese, sugar and peach juice; mix well.Pour mixture on top of peaches.In a small bowl combine sugar and cinnamon together.Sprinkle on top of cream cheese topping.Bake for 30 to 35 minutes.

BUTTERSCOTCH PIE

Ingredients:
1 baked 9 inch pie shell
1 cup brown sugar
4 tablespoons flour
½ teaspoon salt
1 ½ cup milk
3 eggs, separated
2 1/8teaspoons vanilla
3 tablespoons butter
¼ cup granulated sugar

Directions:
In a medium pot over medium to low heat, mix together brown sugar, flour and salt.Add 1 teaspoon of milk to make a paste.Cook until mixture thickens.Remove pot from heat, add 3 egg yolks and the rest of the milk.Place pot back on low heat stirring constantly for 3 minutes or until thick.Remove pot from the heat, add 2 teaspoons vanilla and butter, stir until well mixed.Pour mixture into pie shell and let cool for two hours.

Preheat oven to 400 degrees.In a mixing bowl, beat egg whites until stiff.Add granulated sugar and vanilla and beat until smooth. Spread mixture over pie and bake until meringue is golden brown.

S'MORES PIE

Ingredients:
1 graham cracker pie shell
8 oz marshmallow crème
8 Hershey chocolate bars, unwrapped
1 cup mini marshmallows
1 stick unsalted butter
½ cup granulated sugar
1 egg
1 teaspoon vanilla
1 ½ cups graham cracker crumbs
¾ cup all purpose flour
1 teaspoon baking powder

Directions for Filling Pie:
Preheat oven to 350 degrees.Spread marshmallow crème inside pie shell.Separate 7 whole Hershey bars and place them all over pie bottom.Then sprinkle mini marshmallows on top of Hershey bars.

Directions for Top Crust:
Chop up the remaining Hershey bar in small pieces. In a large mixing bowl, beat butter and sugar together until smooth consistency.Next, add egg and vanilla, mix well.Stir in graham cracker crumbs, flour and baking powder.Mix until firm.Place sections of dough all around the marshmallows but do not cover completely. Top with Hershey bar pieces.Bake for 20 minutes until lightly browned.

CHEESECAKE PIE

Ingredients:
1 graham cracker pie crust
2 packages of cream cheese, softened
1 cup sugar
3 eggs
¼ cup heavy cream
¼ cup sour cream
2 teaspoons vanilla

Directions:
Bake oven to 350 degrees.In a large mixing bowl, combine cream cheese and sugar.Beat in one egg at a time until creamed together.Mix in heavy cream, sour cream and vanilla.Mix until creamy.Pour mixture into pie pan.Bake for 25 to 30 minutes.Cool pie completely, at least 1 hour.Refrigerate overnight.

Note: Can be served with a strawberry, blueberry or raspberry topping.

KEY LIME PIE

Ingredients:
1 graham cracker pie crust
3 eggs, separated
1 egg, slightly beaten
3 cups sweetened condensed milk
½ cup sour cream
½ cup fresh key lime juice
1 teaspoon grated lime zest
whipped cream for garnishing

Directions:
Preheat oven to 350 degrees.Bake pie crust for 5 minutes and let cool.In a medium mixing bowl, whisk 3 egg yolks and beaten egg together.Add in condensed milk, sour cream, lime juice and zest; beat until slightly thickened.

In a separate mixing bowl, beat egg whites until peaks form.Fold egg whites into the custard a little at a time.Pour mixture into pie crust and bake for 15 minutes.Cool completely and refrigerate overnight. Garnish with whipped cream.

SHOOFLY PIE

Ingredients:
1 deep dish pie shell
¾ cup light molasses
¾ cup hot water
¾ tablespoon baking soda
1 egg, beaten
1 ½ cups all purpose flour
¼ teaspoon cinnamon
1/8 teaspoon nutmeg
1/8 teaspoon ginger
1/8 teaspoon cloves
1 cup light brown sugar
¼ cup shortening

Directions:
Preheat oven to 400 degrees.In a medium bowl combine molasses, hot water, and baking soda. Mix well.Whisk in beaten egg.Pour mixture into pie shell.

In a medium bowl combine flour, cinnamon, nutmeg, ginger, cloves and brown sugar. Mix well and cut in shortening until mixture resembles crumbs.Sprinkle crumb mixture on top of molasses layer.Bake for 15 minutes then lower temperature to 350 degrees and bake for additional 30 minutes.

BLUEBERRY PIE

Ingredients:
2 rolled pie crusts
¾ cup white sugar
3 tablespoons clear jel
¼ teaspoon salt
½ teaspoon cinnamon
5 cups fresh blueberries
2 tablespoons lemon juice
1 tablespoon butter, cut in pieces
¼ cup buttermilk

Directions:
Preheat oven to 375 degrees.Line a deep pie dish with 1 pie crust then place blueberries in pie dish.In a medium bowl, combine sugar, clear jel, salt, and cinnamon and sprinkle over blueberries.Add lemon juice and butter pieces on top of blueberries.
Place the other pie crust on top and pinch together. Brush top crust with buttermilk.
Cut 3 slits in the middle of pie and bake for 45 to 50 minutes or until crust is golden brown.

Note: To make a lattice top crust, cut pastry into ¾ in wide strips, crimp and flute the edges.

Clear jel substitutions:1 ½ tablespoons clear jel = 1 tablespoon cornstarch

GOB MINI PIES

Ingredients:
1 cup shortening
2 cups sugar
2 eggs
1 cup buttermilk
4 cups flour
2 teaspoons baking soda
1 teaspoon vanilla
1 cup unsweetened cocoa
1 cup of hot coffee

Directions:
Preheat oven to 375 degrees.In a large mixing bowl, combine shortening, sugar, eggs and buttermilk. Add in flour 1 cup at a time and mix together.Add in baking soda and vanilla. Ina small mixing bowl, combine the cocoa and coffee until cocoa has dissolved in coffee.Pour coffee mixture into batter.Mix well.Drop mixture from a teaspoon onto a greased cookie sheet about 1 to 1 ½ in apart. (You can also use parchment paper).Bake at 375 degrees for 8 minutes.
Cool completely.

Filling:
1 box powdered sugar
1 pint marshmallow cream
3 ½ sticks butter

In a large mixing bowl, combine powdered sugar, marshmallow cream and butter.Using an electric beater, beat mixture until smooth.

Assembling the pies:
Spread a rounded tablespoon of filling on flat sides of half pies and top with remaining half pies.

HULA PIE

Ingredients for Pie:
19inch Oreo pie crust
1 half gallon of vanilla ice cream
1 cup macadamia nuts, chopped
2 cups fudge sauce
whipped cream for garnishing
macadamia nuts for garnishing

Ingredients for Fudge Sauce:
14 oz sweetened condensed milk
1 package semi-sweet chocolate chips
½ cup light corn syrup
1 teaspoon vanilla
1 shot espresso (optional)

Directions for Pie:
Remove ice cream from freezer and allow to soften for 10 minutes.Do not let it melt.When ice cream has softened, remove from container and place in mixing bowl.Mix on low speed until ice cream reaches a thick yogurt consistency.(A standing mixer will work as well using the dough hook attachment)Add in macadamia nuts and mix for one more minute.

Line a medium bowl, with a 9 inch or smaller rim, with plastic wrap and non stick spray.Place ice cream mixture into bowl and let freeze for several hours or overnight.Remove ice cream and pie crust from freezer.Place ice cream mixture into pie crust.(You can turn bowl upside down if it is easier).

Top ice cream with fudge sauce and macadamia nuts.

Directions for Fudge Sauce:
In a medium sauce pan, combine condensed milk, chocolate chips and corn syrup.Cook over medium heat until chocolate is melted and sauce thickens.Remove from heat and stir in vanilla and espresso.Let cool.

Note: If you want fudge sauce to harden, place pie back in freezer until fudge becomes firm.

CHOCOLATE STRAWBERRY PIE

Ingredients:
1 rolled pie crust
1 cup semi-sweet chocolate chips, melted
6 cups fresh strawberries, sliced in half
1 cup granulated sugar
4 ½ tablespoons clear jel
1/2 cup water
1 package dream whip
½ cup milk
½ teaspoon vanilla extract
1 Hershey bar, shaved (for garnish)

Directions:
Preheat oven to 350 degrees.Roll pie crust into a greased deep dish pie pan and bake for 10 minutes until lightly browned.Let cool.Melt the chocolate chips until smooth.

Pour the melted chocolate into cooled pie crust, just enough to cover the bottom and sides. Refrigerate until chocolate hardens.

Arrange 4 cups of strawberries in the chocolate pie shell.Mash the remaining 2 cups of strawberries well. In a medium sauce pan over medium heat, combine mashed strawberries and sugar together.Stir frequently.

In a small bowl, combine clear jel and water; mix well.Gradually pour in clear jel mixture into strawberry mixture.Reduce heat and let simmer until mixture thickens.About 10 minutes. Pour mixture on top of strawberries in pie shell. Chill for several hours.

Whipped Topping:

Combine dream whip, milk and vanilla in a small mixing bowl and beat for 4 to 5 minutes until topping has thickened and formed peaks. Place whipped topping on top of pie.Garnish with Hershey bar shavings.

Note: Clear jel substitutions:1 ½ tablespoons clear jel = 1 tablespoon cornstarch

Made in the USA
Columbia, SC
09 November 2024

46081829R00020